Your Personal Brand: Your Power Tool to Build Career Integrity

Your Personal Brand: Your Power Tool to Build Career Integrity

Kevin Iwamoto

ISBN-13: 9781537001302
ISBN-10: 1537001302

CONTENTS

FOREWORD

When I think about personal branding and how to do it right, Kevin Iwamoto is the first person who comes to mind.

It's not just about the packaging – the surface presentation that people see. You have to have substance behind it. You must actively engage with people, show that you care about them and be passionate about whatever you do. Kevin does all of this extremely well.

As Executive Director and Chief Operating Officer of the Global Business Travel Association, I have to serve a lot of competing interests. Sometimes, not everyone agrees with the decisions we make. Kevin understands what that is like. I can think of many times that he's been a great source of counsel, encouraging us to stay true to our vision. He'd proactively reach out and say: "You set a course; don't let the detractors take you off that course."

Kevin is the only person in our association's history to have received both the GBTA President's Award for industry excellence and contributions (2004) and our very exclusive industry Icon Award (2009). While this is very prestigious, Kevin's brand does not scream: "Hey, look at me." Rather, it's about accomplishing meaningful objectives, impacting the industry and truly helping people make a difference.

I like to think Kevin embodies that old truism about success – that it doesn't come overnight and that you have to work very, very hard to effect positive change.

Thank you, Kevin, for being a powerful force in our industry.

-- Michael W. McCormick
Executive Director and COO, GBTA

FOREWORD

My relationship with Kevin spans two careers and two decades. We first met when I was a Vice President and General Manager for American Express. Kevin, who was Senior Global Travel Commodity Manager for Hewlett-Packard, was one of my strategic customers. We lost touch for a while, but then in early 2013, when I became President and CEO of Meeting Professionals International (MPI), I reconnected with Kevin. Since then we've had numerous discussions about the meeting and event industry, Strategic Meetings Management (SMM) and the value of face-to-face meetings.

With his thought leadership, passion for the meeting profession and experience across multiple segments of the hospitality industry, Kevin has indeed been an ideal person to consult with and learn from. And while he is often called the "godfather" of SMM, I believe he has played much more of an active role as its catalyst, innovator and "founding father." In his career, Kevin has transitioned across the hospitality industry and successfully leveraged the supply chain management discipline introduced to corporate travel management in the 1990s to elevate the strategic discipline and focus of the meeting and event segment of hospitality through the application of SMM.

Kevin's character, commitment and tireless efforts to mentor others and promote the value of meetings have had a profound positive impact on the meeting and event industry. He's passionate about helping others, including organizations like MPI – always placing others before anything he wants to achieve himself. He is a tremendous person and a good friend who, through his selfless actions, has cultivated an enduring and enviable personal brand.

I hope you enjoy getting to know Kevin and can benefit from his wealth of knowledge as you read *Your Personal Brand: Your Power Tool to Build Career Integrity.*

-- Paul M. Van Deventer
President & CEO,
Meeting Professionals International

About Kevin Iwamoto

If you ask people in the business travel and meetings and events industries what they think of my friend, Kevin Iwamoto, I believe a lot of them would describe him very positively. You'd hear words like innovator … icon … intelligent … charismatic … ethical … respected … well liked … generous … self-aware.

There is remarkable consistency in the respect and regard that people hold for him, which reflects the unwavering success of his brand.

Few people are able to rise to the top of a single industry, in this case the business travel industry, and become well known and respected as thought leaders and subject matter experts. But Kevin has accomplished this with every career endeavor he's made, including the indelible mark he's made on the meetings and events industry. I'm impressed with the trove of awards and recognition (check out his LinkedIn profile, https://www.linkedin.com/in/keviniwamoto, for the full list) he's received from both these industries – including some rather unique, rare honors:

- 2016's MPI RISE Award – for meeting industry leadership
- 2016's Top Changemakers Award from *MeetingsNet*
- 2015's Gold Magellan Award from *Travel Weekly* – for Best Travel Industry Blog category
- 2014's & 2011's Silver Magellan Award from *Travel Weekly* – for Best Travel Industry Blog category

- 2013's University of Hawaii, Hall of Honors inductee – for lifetime career achievement
- 2009's GBTA Industry Icon Award, the organization's highest award, given infrequently for lifetime achievements and contributions to the business travel industry.

If you study Kevin's résumé, you'll see he's had a diverse career, developing expertise in sales, marketing, procurement, strategic sourcing, mergers and acquisitions, change management, stakeholder management and global category management – and with blue chip companies like Northwest Airlines, Hawaiian Airlines, The Walt Disney Company, Hewlett-Packard, StarCite, ACTIVE Network and Lanyon. And, almost from the beginning of his career, Kevin has held volunteer leadership roles with various charities, industry boards and associations – like the Global Business Travel Association (GBTA), where in 2001 he was elected President & CEO of the Board of Directors. He's also served the GBTA Foundation and Meeting Professionals International (MPI) Foundation.

I first met and got to know Kevin when he was with HP. Most recently he was Vice President of Industry Strategy at Lanyon, where he guided the company's strategy for engaging with buyers, associations and suppliers. He elected early retirement from Lanyon in May of 2016, and is currently a Senior Consultant at GoldSpring Consulting, an independent travel management consultancy. Putting his career skills and expertise to work, he specializes in global procurement, category management, strategic sourcing, meetings and events, Strategic Meetings Management Programs (SMMPs), and SMM Maturity Indexing for programs.

As long as I've known Kevin, he's been in high demand as a published author, subject matter expert, speaker and blogger (he gained notoriety for his industry blog while at StarCite and Lanyon, and he continues writing for *Meetings & Conventions* magazine).

Kevin has successfully followed his internal compass and mastered managing his brand. I consider Kevin to be one of my trusted advisors. He has the innate ability to bring clarity to complex issues, and he reflects the qualities of my own personal brand. Kevin's contributions to the business travel and meetings and events spaces are immeasurable. He has inspired many of us to stretch beyond our comfort zone in creating our own personal brands, which are formed over a lifetime. Without proper care, they can be vaporized overnight. I have no doubt that this book will help you better understand who you are, who you want to be and how you will be remembered through the contributions you choose to make on your journey.

-- Donna Kelliher, Director, Travel & Corporate Services, Dominion,
GBTA Chairman & Past President

The Iwamoto Brand

"Your brand is what people say about you
when you are not in the room."
— Jeff Bezos

The Iwamoto brand. What is it, and why do I want to tell you about it? First off, back when I started my career, I never once thought about a personal brand — much less write about it. But the more I advanced in the business travel industry, the more I became aware of what beliefs and principles were important to me, and it was only natural that I incorporated them into my daily work habits.

I believe that everybody has a brand, and no matter where you are in your career, you're smart if you can recognize it, continuously develop it, articulate it to others and most importantly, live by it. Your personal brand is a powerful statement about who you are, your work ethic and how you get along with others. Your brand is just as important – if not more important – than your career achievements.

When you're thinking about developing a personal brand, create a vision statement – a few concise, crystallized sentences that describe your core beliefs or ethics and demonstrate your commitment to practicing those values. Your vision statement forces you to be consistent in how you treat others, what you say on social media or to the press, even when making career decisions.

My vision statement is: "If you want respect – respect others. When you learn something – share it. When your friends and family need you – be there. Love and live life unconditionally and without regret."

Everything I do reflects that statement. It helps me maintain my brand integrity on both a personal and professional level.

A word about social media: These days, you're responsible for managing your brand on social media, and it's to your advantage if you excel at it. While you can create both personal and professional social media profiles for, say, Facebook and Twitter, your colleagues still have access to them. So avoid posting inappropriate pictures on any channel—no photos of you dancing with a lampshade on your head. Always remind yourself that anything posted via social media could go viral – even if you intended it to be seen only by family and close friends.

Be Authentic

Simply put, be yourself. If you're easy-going and get along with others at home, take that persona to the workplace, too. There's no need to adopt a different personality on the job, say, someone who is very autocratic and uncooperative with team members, because you feel that's the only way you'll get goals achieved or you have a pre-conceived notion of what a leader should personify.

When you're genuine in your dealings with people, you will find it easy to earn their respect. I've always found that being consistently straight up, and at the same time respectful of others, puts people at ease. They come to know very quickly that you can be depended upon to act a certain way, especially in times of stress, heavy workloads and deadlines.

It's important, too, to be authentic if you speak or present (see page 3 for tips). I speak a lot at global conventions, conferences and local Global Business Travel Association (GBTA) and Meeting Professionals International (MPI) chapters. My speaking style reflects my personal style – genuine, a little self-deprecating and with some humor thrown in. After speaking engagements, I've had many people come up to me and tell me how much more they could relate to me because of my authentic style and humor. They often say, "I had no idea how funny you are. I feel like I know you better and you changed this image I had of you as a very serious speaker. You made learning and listening fun."

I'm not saying you should emulate another's style and speaking demeanor. Use what works for you and makes you comfortable. Most importantly, be yourself and let that shine through.

Your Public Face

Being yourself also serves you well if you give speeches at corporate and industry events, or you are sought out by the media for interviews. People are turned off by phony speakers – who may say all the right things but come across as too staged or disingenuous. Here are some tips on adding authenticity to your public face:

1. *Be consistent with your messages, as that impacts your brand credibility and defines who you are and what you represent.*
2. *Be confident with the topic you're speaking about – a great way to eliminate nervousness. You'll come across at ease if you can speak without any PowerPoint® slides or script. Know your content!*
3. *Make eye contact with members of your audience—they'll feel a direct connection with you.*
4. *Insert humor in your presentation whenever possible. You don't have to be a stand-up comic to be funny. You can share humorous personal stories to illustrate a point or topic. I personally use self-deprecating humor—I never make fun of others, only myself.*
5. *Lack confidence in your writing ability? Ask others for help. Hiring a good speech writer who spends time with you and learns about your style and personality will make your speeches more authentic – just like you!*
6. *Maintain friendly but honest relationships with the media, who may come to regard you as a trusted, knowledgeable source (always check with your corporate communications group before speaking with the press).*

I was once approached by a professional speaking coach after an education session I conducted for an MPI chapter. She started giving me unsolicited advice, speaking tips and a critique of my speaking skills. I politely listened to what she had to say because I thought she might share some valuable tips that I could use to improve my skills. Unfortunately, none of it resonated with me. It was all superficial points, e.g. shift your weight every three to five minutes, cock your head occasionally for dramatic effect, resist engaging in self-deprecating humor. I politely thanked her, and then she gave me her card and offered to be my coach (for a fee, of course).

Getting speaking tips from coaches is fine, but not if it affects your authenticity in delivery. In my opinion speaking well and professionally comes with practice and experience. From my perspective, you can be the most polished and articulate speaker in the world, but if your message and subject matter isn't resonating with your audience because you're not coming across authentically, then you've failed as a speaker. I'd rather be authentic and have an audience absorb my message content versus focus on hand gestures, tonal delivery and

3

shifting my body weight. Yes, those elements help all speakers refine their delivery. But at the end of the day, if you fail at delivering your content messaging, you're not an effective speaker – no matter how polished you appear to be.

> **Tips to Gauge Your Speaking Skills**
>
> 1. *Save your speaker scores from every engagement and log them, using a spreadsheet. You can then see your average scores and track how you're trending as a speaker, based on audience feedback.*
> 2. *Study the feedback and determine if it's relevant or superficial. Use only relevant feedback to improve your speaker effectiveness scoring.*
> 3. *If you start to see an upward trend in positive scoring, then you're improving as a speaker. If the scores are flat, you'll need to figure out what's not working. Ask for honest feedback from the audience. It will only help you to improve.*

Your Word is Your Bond

I learned very early on that your word is your badge of honor, and you should always mean what you say. Whether you're a buyer or supplier, sticking to your word is the biggest brand or reputation characteristic you can develop for yourself.

For a corporate travel buyer, the biggest temptation is to overpromise delivery of market share or revenue numbers to a supplier. My advice: Don't embellish your spend or exaggerate your ability to deliver market share. I know many buyers who do that cavalierly – say whatever they need in order to get discounts and concessions. Unfortunately, they often don't deliver what they promise … or they come up short of the target goals because their corporate travel policies don't encourage or mandate that their employees book with preferred suppliers. This is very damaging to your credibility and also to the reputation of your employer. It's a big industry, yes, but everybody talks. One supplier talks to another, and pretty soon the word gets around that you're unreliable. Worst of all, your managed programs have no integrity. Always keep in mind that a lack of integrity will follow you in your career.

For suppliers, your word is your bond, too. You need to move heaven and earth to deliver the discounts or amenities you promise. Yes, there are circumstances when it becomes difficult to deliver, say, when the hotel you work for gets bought by another lodging company. If you work for an airline, perhaps it's when your carrier eliminates key program flights and routes. But even then, the most important thing is to be transparent. Tell your buyers what's going on, the difficulty you've encountered, the roadblock you've come up against. Strive to work together in a transparent and supportive way but, most importantly, be honest. Trust each other enough to work collaboratively, especially when dealing with challenges and changes. When you do so, both parties come away as winners. Or, you can at least feel the best efforts were made to honor the spirit of the agreement.

Final food for thought: You'll likely change employers several times in your career. Remember that your reputation and personal branding will follow you everywhere. If you have developed a successful and positive brand, it will carry forward and give you some prestige with your employer. Conversely, if your reputation and brand is built on negative buzz, you will find it more difficult to find employment, much less keep a job.

Treat People with Respect

Have you ever gone to lunch with a colleague or senior executive who you thought was well mannered and civil, only to observe with horror how they treated the wait staff? I have been to many industry functions with senior executives who've been perfectly charming while conversing with colleagues at the table but then acted like beasts to the wait staff. It made me want to run and hide – such sad and embarrassing behavior.

On planes, I go out of my way to be nice to the flight crew to make up for the rude behavior I witness, often from people in suits and in premium class. They order flight attendants around and don't say "thank you" or show any empathy for the tough job of serving a cabin full of demanding travelers.

Throughout my career, I've made it a point to practice in the workplace what I learned in childhood – to treat others as I would have them treat me. Virtue is its own reward, yes, but boy, has this paid off handsomely for me. I have had the great privilege of earning the respect, and sometimes friendship, of countless co-workers, bosses, industry executives and influencers.

In the office, make it a habit to spend time with those who report to you. Get to know them and learn about their lives. Ask about their family, partners, children and pets. Perhaps there are opportunities to mentor someone or coach them on management skills. Working with others on a project? It's cool to be in charge, but don't be a dictator. Collaborate graciously with others, and make everyone feel like they're contributing valuable time and talent. I always say, "If you want ownership and collaboration, try inclusion."

Being connected to others – for example, through social media and professional networks – will also help spread your name, professional reputation and brand. Make connections with people who hold similar beliefs and values and professional goals. Remember, we're all in this together!

Be a Visionary

In the workplace, whether you report to someone or someone reports to you, you're the CEO of your own brand. Nobody on the planet has a better vested interest in your ethics, beliefs and way of living like you do. So, when you think of your brand – building, promoting or protecting it – start thinking about it on a more entrepreneurial or executive level. Thinking like a CEO when it comes to your brand spurs you to make better choices. It also takes you out of the weeds, which forces you into more of a strategic versus tactical realm.

Thus, you make better decisions about how you act in the workplace, who you network with and how you treat others. You think more about all your goals: where you want to be in one, three or five years; how your brand will help you get there; and how your brand will grow to reflect the better person you'll become. Always remind yourself that you alone are the captain of your ship and CEO of your personal brand.

Dress for Success

That old saying about how first impressions count still rings true in my books. When I first started my career in this industry, I came up through sales, and I dressed in suit and tie because I wanted to present myself as a professional and show respect to customers. I wanted my *outside* appearance to match my *inside* attitude.

Styles and business customs have changed since then. Things are more relaxed. Conference attendees – both men and women – show up to educational sessions and networking functions in chinos and polo shirts. Corporate employees wear jeans to the office, and CEOs sport dress shirts and blazers.

Regardless of what's in or out, you should always dress true to your brand. If you're young and you work for a hip tech firm, where casual is the norm, take that look with you. I have seen plenty of 20-somethings get up on stage and speak, dressed in a T-shirt, jeans and designer sneakers. Then again, if you're an executive for a five-star hotel chain, it's more appropriate for you to dress conservatively – if not a suit, then at least a pressed shirt and slacks with a blazer.

But whatever your age, employer or brand, remember that the way you dress shouldn't distract from your business purpose. Basic cleanliness and modesty are musts. Shower, shave (if you're a man), brush your teeth and comb your hair. For fancy day or evening events, women should take care to dress appropriately for the occasion. Avoid super-short skirts, ultra-tight clothing or outfits that reveal too much.

Always check yourself in the mirror before leaving your home or hotel room to make sure your brand is well represented by the way you're dressed. Pack at least one day before your trip so you have more time to be thorough.

Once, I actually forgot to bring pants! On another occasion, because I was in a rush, I packed what I thought was a pair of black dress shoes, only to find out the right shoe was dark brown and the left was black.

Traveling overseas for business? Remember that different cultures may have stricter dress customs. Find out beforehand what attire is acceptable at the functions your attending. Then, pack and dress accordingly. You don't want to appear as if you're disrespecting your host's culture.

Always read and pay attention to the dress code recommendations from organizers whenever you're speaking or attending a convention. If the dress code is not listed, ask one of the organizers what their recommendation would be, then pack accordingly. If you're ever in doubt about how to dress appropriately for a meeting, function or event, remember that it's better to overdress than underdress.

Don't Believe Your Own Press

I've spent my career building good relationships with the media – both industry and mainstream press. Industry publications like *Business Travel News* and *MeetingsNet* have graciously put me on their covers on several occasions, and I've been interviewed by mainstream news outlets such as Bloomberg Radio, *The Wall Street Journal*, *USA Today*, and even *The New York Times*. In my home, I am grateful to have a room full of industry awards. But my friends tell me that I've remained humble through it all. It's a great compliment and reassures me that I've remained grounded.

How'd that happen? It's because I believe strongly that no matter where you get to in life, you'd be smart to recognize early in your career that you're no different from the next person. It would be tragic if I put so much stock in those awards that I started to believe I was better than everybody else. I don't need to look at awards to remind me who I am. If anything, I'm humbled and inspired to be a better human being and leader.

Interacting with The Media

If your company gives you permission to speak with the media, you need to exercise caution. I learned very quickly to be careful and seek advance approval and guidelines whenever I make comments to the press. Most companies require media-facing staff to take internal media training first before interacting with the press.

Before an interview, ask the reporter you're speaking with to define what "off the record" means to them. Most journalists will keep your comments off the record if you first identify them as such. Some, however, take the view that whatever you say is "on the record." Better to get the rules of engagement squared away upfront.

Another tip: *Don't lie or pretend you know something just to sound good to the reporter. It's okay to say, "I'm sorry, that's not my area of expertise." The writer will respect you for your honesty and integrity.*

When my time comes, I hope my eulogy isn't about my accomplishments and awards. I really hope people share what a good friend and human being I was … that I was always there for them and others. Receiving accolades and recognition is wonderful; it all serves to validate your work and your brand. But it's far more meaningful to have people remember your acts of kindness. This has been my lifelong conviction.

> "The time is always right to do what is right."
> – DR. MARTIN LUTHER KING JR.

Networking - Step Out of Your Comfort Zone

> "Pulling a good network together takes
> effort, sincerity and time."
> -- Alan Collins, author of *Unwritten HR*
> *Rules: 21 Secrets For Attaining Awesome*
> *Career Success In Human Resources*

When you go to industry events, do you tend to hang out with one or two people you know? At the cocktail hour, do you prefer to go it alone – sitting at a table or standing in a corner nursing your drink, checking your phone for new messages? Do you just make a requisite appearance and then slip out of the room?

If you said 'yes' to one or more of the questions above, you're not alone. A 2015 University of Phoenix study[i] found that "working adults and job seekers are either hesitant to network, or are avoiding it altogether." The study found that 53% "do very little or no networking," although 89% believe networking produces benefits.

At your next event, be adventurous. Be proactive. Search out new people to meet. Why expend the energy? By far, networking has been the most effective tool I've used to grow personally and professionally. That same Phoenix University study found that 27% of those who acknowledged skimping on networking have lost out on a job opportunity as a result.

Not ready to manage the room solo? Find a friendly face and tackle the room together. After all, there's strength in numbers, and you'll have more confidence. Nevertheless, don't just stay with your friends, excluding others from conversations. Set a goal to meet a certain amount of new contacts and collect business cards.

Here's an interesting way to introduce yourself and make a connection when someone at a networking event says they only have one business card left: Offer to take a picture of it and give it back. I've had great conversations with people who tell me about their own challenges with networking, especially when they ask for best-practice tips. Bottom line: People like to find common points of interest. So, the sooner you can find those common points, the easier networking becomes.

At some point you may even master the art of efficient networking. I learned from a professional friend who networked a room of about 300 people in 50 minutes flat! His secret is to pick a side of the room when entering and spend no more than two minutes in conversation with each person he meets. Then he moves to the other side of the room. He keeps moving in one big loop until he can quietly exit. The goal is to collect business cards or names for follow-up on LinkedIn after the event. "It's kind of like speed dating for professionals," he told me. This style of networking allows him time to hit another event or go back to his room and relax. I actually tried it myself—it works.

Whatever your networking style, follow up with your new contacts personally via email and/or LinkedIn. If you're consistent, you'll find yourself with a diverse and large contact database that you can leverage for your entire career.

Professional and Personal Rewards

Networking is not just about getting a better job. Through networking, I've met some wonderful people who've generously shared their friendship, knowledge and expertise with me. That has benefitted me tremendously. I'm a better person because I took the time to get to know new people and broaden my relationships with existing contacts.

However, I look upon face-to-face networking as a discipline. There are rules to obey and etiquette to observe. And there's a philosophy behind it all, too: It's all about generosity. Give freely of your time and talent, and you'll reap your best, most valuable relationships.

In a 2015 *Fortune* article[ii], Tom Farley, president of the New York Stock Exchange, expressed this spirit wonderfully. He said networking "is about collecting relationships with interesting or influential people irrespective of the immediate benefit of these relationships." Farley added: "Networking is not transactional, but too often it's approached in such a way. Play the long game and build the network for the sake of building the network."

My Networking Journey

I couldn't possibly count all the networking functions I have been to, but I'll always remember my first, a Northwest Airlines global sales meeting. Hundreds of sales representatives and management from all over the world were there.

The room was big, crowded, and I was very nervous. I was new in the industry, just starting a gig as a sales account manager. Except for some colleagues I hung out with from the Los Angeles district sales office, I didn't know the majority of people in the room. As I maneuvered my way over to a bar station to get a drink, I hurriedly read the badges on the people I passed. At the same time, I tried to make eye contact and introduce myself.

Such a lot to do – and I had to make it look effortless, too. There was no one to guide and help me; it was truly a scary learn-as-you-go experience. When I look back, I remember that I met some very nice people. In fact, many years and career changes later, I am still friends with many of my former Northwest Airlines sales colleagues and leaders. My strategy was to first look for people with whom I had something in common – and I remember seeking out the Hawaii and California sales folks. But beyond that, I sure could have used some guidance on how to network.

Even to this day, people are shocked when they learn that I am uncomfortable at networking and social discourse. I'm much more suited to longer, quality in-depth conversations than short and casual chats. But I've become more efficient in making new contacts and spending quality time in follow-up. Networking is an important tactic for expanding your professional network and brand. Don't skip out on it. Commit to it, and you will have a richer, more rewarding career.

10 Networking Tips

After more than 28 years making new friends at global events and conferences, here are my 10 networking tips:

1. **Make eye contact.** Always look people in the eyes when you introduce yourself. Averting eye contact makes you seem disingenuous and causes awkward moments that leave a negative first impression.
2. **Don't monopolize the conversation.** Yes, you can talk about yourself, but networking is about give and take. Make it a two-way conversation.

3. **Give good hand.** In some areas of the world, like some European countries, you may kiss colleagues on each cheek when meeting. But, if you're unsure how the other person will interpret that, offer a good, firm handshake instead. Also make sure your palms are dry – not moist or wet. That's a real turn-off for a lot of people. If you're afraid of germs, carry hand sanitizer packets, which is much more convenient than running to the bathroom to wash your hands every time you shake another hand!

4. **Keep it professional.** While it's okay to discuss topics outside of work and career issues, be especially careful not to get too deep into your personal life – especially if you're just getting to know someone. Then again, people generally love it when you remember something about their personal lives, like the name of their child or pet. Also, if a person has a name that's difficult to pronounce, take the time and effort to learn how to say it. You'll make a terrific first impression as a caring person.

5. **Be sensitive.** Going to an international event where you expect to meet people from different countries and cultures? Before you arrive, do a little research about the social customs and practices of the host country. Even if you stumble over foreign phrases or make a mistake, your new contacts will appreciate your effort to respect their culture.

6. **Be smooth.** If you're conversing with someone but want to move on, there's a way to do it without being rude. Look for someone you know and draw them into the conversation. Then, politely exit. You've just made an introduction and, at the same time, found a nice way to move on.

7. **Be discreet.** Don't make it obvious you're reading name badges. If you're at an event with no badges (or their name badges are flipped around) and you think you recognize someone but can't remember their name, engage in small talk to buy some time to remember who they are. Another tactic is to ask someone you know at the function if they know the name of the person. If you still draw a blank, then be upfront and politely admit it. Perhaps you can say: "I'm sorry, your first name slipped my mind." If someone's name badge is flipped around, lean over and fix it for them. I do it, look at their name and remark: "There, now everyone can know who you are!" It gets a laugh every time, and people will remember you.

8. **Keep it clean and above the line**. At all costs, avoid raunchy jokes and trashing others. People may think you're mean-spirited, gossipy, immature and insecure – maybe even someone they can't trust.

9. **Avoid debates.** For heaven's sake, stay away from discussing politics, religion and controversial topics that could alienate people. If someone else starts discussing unpleasant topics, listen politely but don't join in. Here's another tip on how to extricate yourself from that kind of a situation: Offer to get drinks for people or seek out a friend passing by and start a conversation with them, thereby exiting gracefully from debate-ridden conversations.

10. **Watch your alcohol intake.** I know it's tempting to overindulge in alcohol at a function, especially with an open bar. However, remember you are attending a professional function, and all eyes are on you. It won't look good if you start behaving badly. Intoxication causes lapses in good judgment and can negatively affect your brand and reputation. I know of several people who didn't get promotions or jobs because the word on the street was they had an alcohol problem. One of my former CEOs used to always stand up at company-wide meetings and remind people about drinking too much. When I was President and CEO of the National Business Travel Association (now the Global Business Travel Association), I wouldn't drink alcohol publicly at any of the official receptions and gatherings because I wanted to remain clear-headed and stay in control of my brand and reputation. After I stepped down, I went to an industry dinner and ordered a cocktail. An airline executive friend said to me, "I didn't know you drink!" I laughed and said: "I'm not a heavy drinker, but I do enjoy a glass or two. That's usually my limit. What made you think that?" She responded: "Because in all the years I watched you as President of NBTA, I never once saw you consume any alcohol." I guess that proves my point that all eyes are on you.

Stay Connected & Relevant with Social Media

A re you among the 1 billion-plus[iii] daily active users of Facebook? Have you joined the army of over 300 million[iv] tweeters? Are you networking with 450 million[v] others on LinkedIn?

Today, interacting on these and other social media platforms is not just a way to pass the time, it's a habit. For example, 72% of online adults in the U.S. use Facebook, and of them, 70% log on daily (43% do so several times a day)[vi]. Social media, including blog writing, is also a great tool for promoting your professional skills and career achievements, as well as sharing your knowledge.

I start each day checking out what's trending and happening on LinkedIn, Twitter and, if I have time, Facebook. Since Facebook tends to be more social for me, I log on and contribute during lunch break and after dinner.

Do you want to use blogs, Facebook, Twitter, Instagram, Snapchat and LinkedIn to post about conferences and events you're attending, promote content you've written or give your point of view on industry events? First things first: Check in with your corporate communications or public relations folks to see if your company policy allows it. If so, what are the guidelines? How much and what type of information about your company can you share?

Blogging: Let Your Knowledge Flow

Before I got into Facebook and Twitter, I started writing a blog when I was with StarCite in 2008. After ACTIVE Network bought StarCite, I continued writing up until 2016, when I retired from my job as VP of Industry Strategy at Lanyon (Vista Equity bought ACTIVE Network in 2014, then merged the

Business Solutions Group with Lanyon, another Vista portfolio company). Frankly speaking, I didn't even know what a blog was, and I was quickly educated by Christine Gallatig Ottow, StarCite's Director of Marketing. I couldn't quite grasp the concept of blogging and questioned why people would care or even take time to read editorial content from me. Not only was that blog a great tool for discussing important industry news, events and trends, it was also the perfect vehicle for me to share my travel and meetings management expertise.

All of my employers loved the blog, too. It lived on their websites, and I could subtly promote upcoming events, product development news and corporate milestones on my professional industry space. The industry trade magazine, *Travel Weekly*, took notice, too. In 2011 and 2013, they awarded me their Magellan Silver Award for "Overall Industry Blog," and then, in 2015, I won the Magellan Gold Award. Today, my blog[vii] is published in *Meetings & Conventions* (www.meetings-conventions.com) magazine, which created a special "Industry Insights" section for me to write about anything I feel I want to express to the industry. It's also published via LinkedIn and resides as part of our consultants' blog section on the GoldSpring Consulting website (www.goldspringconsulting.com).

Worried about what people may think of your writing? Don't. Early in my career, I was responsible for producing a monthly department newsletter for one of my former employers. My boss, however, felt my writing skills were lacking and had me sign up for some outside writing courses.

Well, I basically re-learned everything I had already mastered in college English classes. And, after handing in one of my first essays, our instructor announced I had the best essay. I was in complete shock. I thought, "How can this be? My boss thinks I'm the worst writer."

I told the instructor what my boss thought, and what she said next gave me a whole new perspective on other people's opinions. She laughed and said, "Don't forget that people disliked Hemingway's and Austen's writing. So many popular writers today have been rejected numerous times by book editors everywhere. People's opinions are just that, their opinions. There's a market and audience for anyone wishing to share their talents and views; just remain authentic in what you write and you will be fine."

I've never forgotten her words of advice for me, and I often wonder what my former executive manager would think about my success with writing for the public.

Facebook: Start a Conversation

I've always used Facebook (www.facebook.com/**kevin.m.iwamoto**) to keep my industry network up to speed on my upcoming speaking gigs. I've also posted comments on great business hotels and airline service, attaching pictures or videos (including visuals generates up to 94% more views[viii]). And I've shared tips or lessons from important educational sessions and speeches I've attended at industry conventions.

Your Facebook posts should always elicit conversations – and you can do that simply by asking others their opinions about your topic. Once people start replying, don't forget to "like" their comments, and, if you want, respond.

---

5 Tips for Social Media Use

Here are 5 tips to navigate your way through and get more comfortable with social media:

1. Avoid politics, religion and other personal information and opinions. Share those views with a much smaller and select group of friends and family and NOT with your professional social network.
2. What you post is permanent. Deleting doesn't make embarrassing posts or photos go away. Remember that.
3. Separate your professional social media from your personal to maintain the integrity of your posts.
4. If you're sensitive about data privacy, remember that your posts, opinions and photos will always find its way to the mainstream. HR departments often use social media to build a profile on prospective candidates for jobs, since they are heavily restricted from asking personal questions during interviews. If you are seeking employment or want to stay employed, be responsible!
5. In this age of social transparency, you should never utter these words to a new contact: "So, tell me about yourself and your company." With social media and the internet available for professional and personal research, that question immediately says, "I'm too lazy to have researched you and your company." Not a good first impression.

Twitter: Content is King

I love Twitter (@KevinIwamoto) because it's a form of instant communication with those I follow and who follow me. I can tweet from conferences and events, giving my impressions of speakers – all as it's happening real-time.

You've got to be brief with your tweets—140 characters is the limit. So make what you say count – and for me that means making sure I include a link

(I shorten links via Ow.ly and Bitly.com) to content residing on my blog. I love the challenge of condensing my tweets; it's made my overall communication and messaging much more succinct and to the point.

Adding photos and videos catches your followers' attention, as there's a constant stream of tweets coming in. And, you can give your tweets expanded attention and viewership by including hashtags (#) before key industry and social terms, for example, #GoWarriors, #SMMP (Strategic Meetings Management Program) and #biztravel. Also, if you're attending a conference, say, the GBTA convention, don't forget to include the conference hashtag (#GBTA2016).

It's mind-boggling how Twitter can help you greatly expand your audience. You can even leverage statistics on your follower totals when negotiating fees for speaking appearances or endorsements for your products or merchandise.

LinkedIn: Join Groups, Advance Your Career

I like LinkedIn because it's a great way to connect with other folks in our industry, join and contribute comments (and blog posts) to industry groups, as well as update my profile with new career information. My LinkedIn profile (https://www.linkedin.com/in/keviniwamoto) is where I list all my industry milestones and awards. I also participate in several industry groups and frequently check to see what is trending and being discussed.

Another great thing about LinkedIn: It's a good platform to search for job opportunities (click on the Jobs tab to find postings). There's even a premium membership geared toward finding a job.

Often, corporate recruiters will look at your profile as they search to fill positions at their companies. If you include an email and phone number in your profile, it's easier for them to contact you. Actually, LinkedIn is the most popular place for recruiters to mine job candidates (87% of recruiters[ix] use LinkedIn).

Make Your Social Media Life Easy!

I use the free version of Hootsuite.com, a central hub where I can post to and manage all my social accounts. There's even a neat tool that allows you to schedule posts for the future – so that you can keep active on social media while you're away on business or vacation. Plus, an analytics tool tells you which content resonates most with your audience.

LinkedIn is also the best place to demonstrate your thought leadership by regularly posting and publishing content. Keep it professional, though, by resisting posting overt sales and social-focused commentary (use Facebook, Instagram and Snapchat for social-oriented content). You can successfully establish your personal brand via LinkedIn if you leverage the medium appropriately.

Being Responsibly Social

Social media has definitely changed the way we live. Now, we can more easily communicate with each other and express our individuality. Be consistent. Be who you are. But be responsible and aware. To me, the pros far outweigh the cons, but the responsibility for your actions is 100% on you.

I'm always amazed at the amount of personal information that is publicly shared online via social media, especially Facebook and Twitter. If you have a combined personal/professional account on both Facebook and Twitter, then you have to really exercise good judgment and discernment concerning the posts you create and pictures you post. If your account is purely personal, you have a lot more leeway, but you should still exercise good judgment because it can be viewed and accessed publicly. Also with every bit of information you put out there, you could be giving identity thieves and burglars license to do you harm both financially and physically. So exercise caution and don't divulge too much online.

I also make it a habit to periodically search my name on Google, Bing, Yahoo and other search engines to find out if someone has mentioned me or re-purposed something I've written. I'd say that 99% of the time the mentions of my work are positive; for example, some publication in Indonesia re-publishing an interview with me. But if you find something objectionable, by all means follow up with that person to discuss. For example, if they failed to credit you for your original thought piece, ask them to do it immediately. Auditing your online presence also helps you to keep on top of how the media is covering you and how your external brand is being represented.

I have to thank and acknowledge my late brother-in-law, Marvin Wong, for making me aware of search engines. He said he was impressed with the number of pages in Google and other search engines that referenced my name from media clips. I had no clue what he was talking about until he showed me, and I was amazed and have been checking my personal brand online ever since.

Another tip: Buy up your domain names so you can protect your brand (GoDaddy.com offers cheap domain names on top-level domains ".com" and ".net"). This is a wise move in case you want to run for office or open your own business. I regret not moving fast enough to buy up the "Kevin I" domain when I was a professional singer. That was my stage name way back in my younger days, and I intended to create a website where I could sell and post music and photos. But the domain was already taken. Years later, I was able to buy and register it with the other domains I have. So, one day I'll have the luxury of building personal websites at my leisure.

Also, remember this rule of thumb: The internet and social media are wonderful because they're 24/7 and immediately global. The downside to the internet and social media is that they're 24/7 and immediately global. Try to remember this, especially if you're using your mobile phone and have had a few drinks or are tired and sleep-deprived. Have a clear mind before posting anything online and you won't have any unpleasant surprises later.

Always think before you post!

Make an Investment in Continuing Education—You're Worth It!

> "Let us never be betrayed into saying we
> have finished our education; because that
> would mean we had stopped growing."
> -- Julia H. Gulliver

D o you ever wonder how it would look to have credentials behind your name – those impressive capital letters that signify you are recognized for possessing special knowledge of a subject or discipline? Maybe you think you need to spend a lot of money and time pursuing them. Or, perhaps you think you need to go away for a long time to a university to earn them.

Not necessary – on both counts. I know because I've got a few of those letters behind my name: Global Leadership Professional® (GLP) Program and Global Travel Professional® (GTP) Certification. I worked hard to earn them. But I enjoyed every minute of those experiences, got a head full of new knowledge, and met great people.

My first was the GLP certification. I decided to go for it while I was working for Hewlett-Packard (HP), which offered me a continuing education subsidy. GLP is the only master's-level course for travel professionals offered by the Global Business Travel Association (GBTA) in conjunction with The Wharton School, The University of Pennsylvania. I received invaluable education in management, marketing, leadership and finance. And, while I did have to travel to Philadelphia for a full week for some on-campus core instruction at Wharton, I completed my GLP over the course of nine months, taking remote electives and working with a team of other industry professionals. Our team met virtually and in person, culminating in a full documentation of our group thesis findings—we presented it live at GBTA. The best part was that my out-of-pocket costs were minimal due to a scholarship I received from GBTA and the supplemental continuing education funding from HP.

Ask – You Just Might Receive

When I decided to go for my GLP, it was a very financially challenging year for HP, and they were not giving any raises and bonuses. Maybe a lot of people might not even ask for assistance when their company isn't performing well. But I thought, "It doesn't hurt to ask the question." I did, and my manager agreed to find out if it was possible. As it turned out, the continuing education budget was intact. The bottom line: Don't be afraid to ask your employer for financial assistance; the worst they can do is say "No."

For my GTP, I studied and worked with other travel professionals in my local GBTA chapter, the Silicon Valley Business Travel Association (SVBTA). Testing is a big part of the GTP certification, which the GBTA says aims to "elevate professional standards and recognize individuals who demonstrate the knowledge essential to the practice of the business travel profession." You have to pass the initial test, which measures a comprehensive knowledge of the industry. Then, to keep the certification, you have to take the test again every three years.

Looking back, getting my GTP was, in some respects, very stressful. I had to carve out time from my job to study and meet with my fellow students. And, let's face it, who likes taking a test? But because my employer at that time, ACTIVE Network, fully supported my decision to pursue this designation, I was able to study and get together with my fellow study group members after work. It was a great experience, and the friendships I made in that group transcended the whole experience and bonded us together. I am happy to say a lot of those friendships I made are still intact today, especially since we all passed!

Go for Those Letters

Do you want to get professional accreditations but doubt your ability to afford it financially or time-wise? Concerned the tests might be too tough? Don't worry—you can do it! Getting accredited will very likely propel your career forward (those letters follow you no matter where you go!), and it will enrich you personally.

Consider a designation like CPA, MBA, PHD, CPM and especially something universally recognized, such as Six Sigma or Lean Six Sigma green or black belt. A designation of expertise around Six Sigma is universally recognized no matter what your vocation. Having that knowledge, skill set and designation also makes you a more desirable job candidate. Here's proof: As of May 2016, the median annual Six Sigma Black Belt salary in the US was $102,312, with a range between $93,221 and $109,989, according to Salary.com research.[x]

If you're a meeting planner, a Certified Meeting Planner (CMP) designation from the Convention Industry Council will earn you $8,500 per year more than those without it, according to Professional Convention Management Association (PCMA) research[xi].

The decision to invest time and money into designations and accreditations is totally up to you. From my own experience, I can tell you that my salary negotiations were always successful because of my accreditations. It automatically started the compensation conversations with employers at a higher baseline.

Here are 5 tips to consider when going for an accreditation:

1. **Get lettered for your passion.** Go after credentials that support what you do best and that are meaningful in your industry. Studying something you love will keep you engaged during the course. And, when you've passed and received recognition, it will speak volumes about your professional commitment to present and future employers. Before undertaking the time and expense in studying for any certification, do some research and decide what accreditations will support your career goals and objectives. For example, if you are a meeting planner and are researching a Certificate in Meeting Management (CMM) or CMP designation, but your goal is to move out of meeting planning and into project management, you may be better off investing in a Project Management Professional (PMP) certification – even a black or green belt in Six Sigma.

2. **Get industry help paying for it.** Many industry associations offer members scholarships to help pay for education. For example, GBTA Foundation has several partners that provide scholarships for its GLP program. In addition, some of the GBTA chapters and affiliates

provide scholarships to their members for various educational programs. Surprisingly, there are many scholarships both on the national and local levels that go unclaimed. Do some research and apply!

3. **Use your corporate benefits.** When you start thinking about continuing your education, sit down with your manager to determine whether your company can give you some time off to attend classes, study and take tests. If the accreditation you're considering supports your specialty, and if you can make sure your work gets done (don't be afraid to delegate work to others), there's a good chance they'll support you. Also, meet with your corporate benefits manager to check out what kind of financial underwriting is available for continuing education. Just make sure you understand all of the rules and obligations for the financial aid. For example, your employer may require you to continue to work for a designated period of time to ensure they can benefit from your continuing education and leverage their financial investment in your designation.

4. **Join a study group.** Don't be afraid to reach out and create study-buddy groups with fellow applicants. It's great to be able to get together with others, expand your network, share ideas and figure stuff out together. An added benefit is that some of those students could be future clients or valuable contacts for a new job.

5. **Pay forward what you've learned.** You'll be doing the industry a favor if you can share your new knowledge with others. Write a piece on something you've learned for your internal newsletter. Or, take it outside and contact an editor from an industry trade magazine for submission. Tell editors that you're available for quotes (if your company policy allows) or case studies.

For more information on accreditation courses for both business travel and meetings and events, contact:

- GBTA – Tel: 703-684-0836/Email: academy@gbta.org
- Meeting Professionals International (MPI) – Tel: 972-702-3000/ Email: cmm@mpiweb.org

Giving – The Secret to Being a Successful Human

> "If having a soul means being able to feel
> love and loyalty and gratitude, then animals
> are better off than a lot of humans."
> -- James Herriot

One of my favorite quotes comes from one of the most admired women in the world –Saint Teresa, a Roman Catholic nun who devoted her life to serving the poor and destitute around the world. She said: "It is not the magnitude of our actions but the amount of love that is put into them that matters."

What a great saying! It reflects my own desire to give what I can to causes that touch my heart. I don't have to have the resources of Facebook's Mark Zuckerberg to give back – both personally and professionally – to society. I just have to give what I can. It can be time. It can be money. It can be knowledge. Maybe it's all three. But there has to be passion involved. I need to believe in whatever I'm committing myself to.

Pay Career Blessings Forward

I think it's very important to pay forward some of the good fortune others have bestowed upon you in the workplace. I've certainly tried to practice this over the course of my career.

I graduated from the University of Hawaii, Honolulu, (UH) with a Bachelor of Science degree in Business Administration. And that was only possible because I received a four-year scholarship from Hawaiian Airlines, where I was working part time (in addition to singing at night at a local dance club). The scholarship helped me gain the knowledge I needed to enter the workforce and start my career.

Hawaiian Airlines also helped me realize a childhood dream. As a kid, I would look at pictures of far-away places in my geography textbook, stare out the window and dream that one day I'd see those sites. I remember going to the Honolulu International Airport and watching the planes take off for exotic destinations, fantasizing about being on those planes and having my own travel adventures. Working for Hawaiian Airlines, and later Northwest Airlines, I got to see some of this world's most beautiful, diverse places – and to experience fascinating, exotic cultures.

That kind of blessing needs repaying. So, in 2013, I established a perpetual scholarship at UH's School of Travel Industry Management (TIM) for students interested in a career in the hospitality industry. Full funding for this scholarship will become available for student application in 2018. I'm proud to know that future students at the UH TIM School will benefit with a little extra help from my scholarship.

In 2016, I set up another scholarship – this one with Meeting Professionals International (MPI). I started this one for a very different reason. As a third-generation Japanese American, I want to encourage diversity of future leaders in the meeting and travel industry. The MPI scholarship is open to applicants of ethnic diversity who are interested in pursuing a career in the meeting and event industry and covers association membership, access to the MPI job bank and other invaluable resources.

What the Workplace Needs Now: More Diversity

I was blessed that I was raised in Hawaii – an ethnic melting pot. It was only when I moved to the mainland U.S. to pursue my career that I learned about racial prejudice, profiling and denial of opportunities. I personally never allowed myself to buy into "glass ceiling" limitations, and I managed to have a successful career.

I believe strongly that we need more diversity in positions of leadership in our industry. Yes, the current leadership looks a lot different now than 15 years ago, when I started my term as president & CEO of the Global Business Travel Association (GBTA). There certainly are a lot more women in leadership roles. But, at this writing, I am still the only ethnic minority to have ever held the top position at GBTA. I sit on industry boards where, again, I am the only Asian American or one of very few ethnically diverse members.

Diversity is a good thing because it helps us broaden our perspectives. We learn from other people's experiences. We can then incorporate their input and needs into our educational programs and mission statements. As a result, we attract wider, broader audiences. Ultimately, we all grow. Companies and boards should appoint the most qualified individuals regardless of their ethnicity. That is why it's so important to give minorities and women opportunities to become the best they can be so they are fully qualified and, most importantly, ready to take that important step to the upper echelon of management and leadership.

One bright, shining area of opportunity that exists with no glass ceiling is the online world (see text box on page 28). Plus, corporations are making some effort to reduce the negative impact of the glass ceiling on women and minority leaders. But, there's still much more work that needs to be done. For example, the pay gap that exists between men and women working the same jobs needs to be addressed by governance and compensation boards (A 2016 article in *The Wall Street Journal*[xii] reported that, across occupations, American women earn 79% of men on average).

I once was interviewed by a media publication that called out my status as a groundbreaker in the travel and meeting industry, and my response to that statement was never published. But it went something like this: Maybe I was successful in breaking new ground but that was never intentional. I never acknowledged or accepted any glass ceiling in anything I did or aspired to do throughout my career. I pushed forward without any regard for any gatekeepers, obstacles or stereotypes of who and what people thought I should be. I was fortunate to choose to work in the travel and meeting industry, which is very liberal and, for the most part, blind to discrimination targeting a person's gender, race and sexual orientation.

> **Social Media Helps Break Barriers**
>
> *The digital age has diversified the marketplace with astounding speed. Take Michelle Phan, a beautiful Asian-American millennial who is a makeup demonstrator and entrepreneur. She loves cosmetics so much that she created her own YouTube channel and has over 8 million subscribers and 1.1 billion lifetime views. In 2013, L'Oréal launched "em," a cosmetics line by Michelle Phan, who dedicated the brand to her mother. In 2015, Phan was named to Inc. magazine's "30 Under 30" list. She also made the "Forbes 30 Under 30" list. The same year, Phan raised $100 million to value her company, Ipsy, at over $500 million. Phan is just one of many who never accepted the glass ceiling and made a success of herself.*

I predict the next generation will smash all remnants of the glass ceiling, and it will become a footnote in history books. Until then, my advice is to not let others define, stereotype or restrict you. Be yourself. Love who you are, and teach others to be more tolerant and accepting of all. By being the best you can be, you are showing others that their own pre-conceived biases are wrong.

One of my favorite quotes about this comes from television personality Ellen DeGeneres: "Find out who you are and be that person. That's what your soul was put on this Earth to be. Find that truth, live that truth, and everything else will come." I have this quote posted at my desk. Such great inspiration from such a genuinely wonderful person!

Build Support for Your Causes

Giving back is not only good for the soul, it gives others insight into your character and your beliefs. Your charitable works are powerful personal brand-builders, too!

I'm passionate about helping our military veterans and caring for animals in trouble. And I've been lucky enough to build more support for those causes at the workplace and in my personal life.

It's my belief that we don't do enough as a nation to honor and help veterans and their families after they've made incredible sacrifices to protect our country. On the other hand, I don't feel like it's the government's responsibility 100%, either. I feel strongly that every citizen should be thankful to our veterans and contribute in some way to help them. Maybe it's helping them find jobs. Or perhaps it's donating time or money to charities like Wounded Warrior Project® (www.woundedwarriorproject.org) and other organizations that support veterans. What a tragedy that we have homeless veterans living on the streets. They're not receiving the care and help they deserve after serving our country. As a nation we can do so much better.

Build Support for Your Personal Charities

1. *Share articles or posts about charitable events* on social media. Avoid telling people they "must" donate or join. Instead, simply bring information to their attention, and then let them make up their own minds.

2. *Get corporate support.* Talk with your company's Human Resources department and your CEO, and ask to add your pet cause to your company's social responsibility agenda. That way everyone in your organization will become aware of your cause, and maybe they'll help out.

3. *Team up with co-workers.* Promote each other's charitable causes. For example, sponsor each other in fun-runs or give to charity drives. Give each other a boost on social media, too.

Gofundme.com (www.gofundme.com) is a good tool for crowdfunding and fundraising.

You don't have to donate a lot of money, either. For example, if you see soldiers at a coffee shop or fast-food joint, buy their drinks or meals -- anonymously. I guarantee you'll feel great after doing this simple gesture. On planes, I've seen people give up their first-class seats for active-duty military personnel. I always try to thank them for their service and sacrifices for our freedom. Do what you can, when you can. Even the smallest gesture counts.

Another cause I'm passionate about is caring for animals. It breaks my heart to see animals suffering, especially at the hands of humans. They have no voice, and so I lend mine – chiefly by giving to causes like the American Society for the Prevention of Cruelty to Animals (ASPCA) and The Humane

Society. To honor my beloved Akita, Kimo, I also support the TikiHut Akita Rescue Association (www.tikihutakitarescue.com) which rescues, rehabilitates and finds homes for Akitas. The Akita breed has the longest recorded history of cooperating and working with humans, in this case in Japan. They are considered special and noble for their loyalty and intelligence. Everyone who has ever shared a home with an Akita realizes how special they are. So all Akita dogs deserve to have homes where they can give their unconditional love and support to their human partners.

Regardless of your charities or causes, there are a lot of opportunities out there to be a better human being and corporate citizen. Give back. Pay it forward. Your reward is knowing you're helping to make the world a better place before you leave it.

"If you can't feed a hundred people, then feed just one."
- SAINT TERESA

COMPETING – TAKE THE HIGH ROAD

"I have been up against tough competition all my
life. I wouldn't know how to get along without it."
-- WALT DISNEY

Many times in both your professional and personal lives, you'll encounter competition. It's a challenge, yes. But the best thing you can do is to first accept it and then determine how you want to manage through it.

When faced with competition, some practice a winner-takes-all approach and decimate all in their path to get to the top. Some actually thrive from competition. They don't know how to progress without it, and they use it as a catalyst for achieving their personal best. If they're not competing, they don't achieve anything.

Then again, there are those, like myself, who use self-competition as a way to stay on top of their game. For me, this means setting ambitious but attainable targets and goals for myself – based on what I want to achieve, not because I'm trying to outdo others.

Living in a vibrant environment helps if you're self-driven. I live in Silicon Valley, California—the intense competition for jobs and survival keeps me on top of my game and doesn't allow me to get lazy or complacent. Unfortunately, some people are consumed, even obsessed, by competition. They think they need to win at all costs, pretty much ruining their relationships with colleagues and co-workers and damaging their personal brands. I've seen it happen so many times throughout my career.

I, too, have made mistakes from over-competing, and I've learned valuable lessons from the experiences that have helped me avoid repeating the same behavior. There was a time, early in my sales career, when some of my colleagues stopped talking to me. It bothered me so much that I asked someone I felt close to why people weren't engaging with me as usual. She then shared that my drive for perfection was being perceived as unrealistic competition with my colleagues, and they felt intimidated and threatened by my behavior.

That was the *last* thing I was trying to do. I was being competitive with myself and unknowingly making my colleagues uncomfortable and resentful towards me. Since that experience, I've made a mental note to always be sensitive to the feelings and rights of others. I went from outwardly competing to being inclusive and collaborative. Now, I test myself by asking others to let me know if they are feeling otherwise.

The lesson learned: I may think my behavior is fine, but the people around me may not think so. It pays to ask others for their feedback.

Here are four tips on how to manage competition:

1. **Do some introspection.** Try to figure out if you are displaying unhealthy and obsessive competitive traits that could damage your personal brand. If so, you need to dig deep and be honest with your self-assessment. If you are still unclear or in denial, ask some trusted friends, colleagues and family members to share their impressions of your competitive side. Is it damaging or hurtful? Has it made you prioritize your life in an unhealthy way, like putting in too many work hours, always trying to be first and better than others, bragging about your accomplishments? Find out what others are feeling and how they perceive you. It will at least enlighten you about your reputation and brand.

2. **Celebrate and be proud of the accomplishments of others.** Don't feel threatened. Doing this consistently will tone down any competitive urges you may have. There's far more joy and sense of family when everyone celebrates wins and successes versus singularly celebrating an accomplishment. The best executives surround themselves with people that are smarter and more talented than them. They could easily take the competitive road and surround themselves with people they can intimidate and belittle. In time, they'll bring about their own demise, as they'll be surrounded by "yes" people. All innovation and

successes will be hollow and empty. Don't compete. Collaborate and celebrate.

3. **Avoid the negative talk, gossip, lying and scheming.** We've all encountered and worked with people who engage in this behavior. It's so easy to succumb to it, too, especially when we feel threatened or intimated. Avoid it and people who personify this behavior at all costs, as you'll be sabotaging your karma. People who use this tactic to get ahead of the competition eventually find themselves on the receiving end of this negative behavior. I've actually seen people get transferred or terminated because they were viewed as "bad apples." This is the worst type of self-branding, and your career trajectory could be seriously impaired if you're generally viewed as a negative, competitive person. In cases where it's difficult to remove yourself from the situation, always endeavor to take the high road and decline participation in the negativity.

4. **Compete with yourself not others.** By competing with yourself and not others, you will improve your skills and achieve your goals. This means believing in yourself and trusting in your abilities. Try to be reasonable, and set attainable targets and personal limits to avoid becoming obsessive about the goals you set for yourself. Imagine what you can accomplish by being the best that you can be – by challenging and competing with yourself! Just make sure that your self-competition isn't perceived incorrectly by your family and colleagues. You can do your own self-assessment by asking those around you if your personal competition is negatively impacting them.

"Live daringly, boldly, fearlessly. Taste the relish to be found in competition – in having put forth the best within you."
-- HENRY J. KAISER

PERSONAL BRAND DAMAGE CONTROL

"In my own experience, both personally and
professionally, I've learned that you don't wait to
confront reality. It doesn't get easier. It doesn't get
better. And, in some cases, if you don't get the relevant
information from people and act quickly, you start
losing options. You're into damage control."

-- STEPHEN COVEY

We live in an age where your professional or personal mistakes and misjudgments can quickly become known by your extended network – even by the media. Your personal identity and life are online and can be found via social media or a simple internet search. Today, news publications routinely quote political figures' tweets and broadcast bystanders' cell phone videos. The tools to turn a private moment into a public one are everywhere – smart phones, tablets and CCTV cameras positioned in public spaces.

Even if you're not a public figure such as a high-profile business executive, professional athlete or politician, your brand can take a hit with one little slip-up. Repercussions to your career will haunt you unless you do some quick personal brand repair.

I love what Michelle Ragsdale (https://www.linkedin.com/in/michelle-ragsdale), who directed public relations when I worked at ACTIVE Network and who is now an independent communications and PR consultant, advises: "When a crisis occurs, the most important first step is to not panic. Instead, pause and take a deep breath. Then, take another deep breath before you do anything. There is no sense making a crisis bigger than it is because you panicked and let your emotions dictate your response."

Based on professional advice I gathered, here are five best practices to consider when repairing your personal brand:

1. **You did it—now own it.** Here's where your character needs to be front and center. It starts with taking personal accountability. Don't blame others, the circumstances, being under the influence of alcohol or drugs or some other excuse. Just own it and apologize … period. Excuses only serve to further damage your credibility and character. People will accept and respect you more if you admit your own indiscretions and accept responsibility for your actions.

2. **Talk about what happened.** Silence is never golden when it comes to brand control. You have to think through and design a solid statement, and then articulate it. Do it as fast as possible, too. Keep what you say short, factual and sincere. Anything stated beyond that could backfire on you. Less is better.

3. **Re-define your personal brand**. You will need to be consistent and remind people of what your brand is and what values you want to repair publicly. Set goals and be laser-focused on what you need to say and do in order to get people believing in your personal brand again. From this point on, there's no room for errors and mistakes. Be consistent, and only do and say things that reinforce and remind people of the positive aspects of your personal brand. It will take time, but your social and professional network – the public, too – will love that you've said your mea culpa and come back stronger than before. This has happened before, and can happen for you if you're genuinely contrite and consistent after your apology.

4. **If you are too distracted or distraught, invest in the professionals.** Research and hire experts in personal branding, public relations, social media, marketing and image consulting. For this option, price shouldn't be your primary concern. It should be how quickly the professional team comes up with a plan and then speed-to-market. Remember, the longer you take to repair your brand, the more the situation becomes your new norm.

5. **Measure your campaign results.** Whether you hire professionals or not, you can check to see if your damage control campaign is working by monitoring your name and profile on social media and search engines. You should check this daily, and when you see the dialog about you diminishing or public opinions changing to a more positive tone, then you'll know your damage control campaign is working.

I could list a lot of famous people whose careers and lives were ruined by their past actions, youthful innocence and naiveté, poor decisions, too many drinks or because they were given bad advice. Rather, let's focus on the positive and consider all of the celebrities and public figures who've suffered through bad press and handled their damage control well enough to continue enjoying successful careers. Top of mind are Vanessa Williams, Britney Spears, Hugh Grant and Robert Downey Jr. The message of hope from these celebrity experiences: The public generally likes to forgive and offer support, but only if the offender's apology is sincere and their future behavior and words reflect the lessons learned.

> "You have control over three things - what you think, what you say, and how you behave. To make a change in your life, you must recognize that these gifts are the most powerful tools you possess in shaping the form of your life."
> - SONYA FRIEDMAN

Great Leadership = Passion for Service

"Leadership is not about titles, positions, or flowcharts.
It is about one life influencing another."
-- John C. Maxwell.

When I think of some of the world's most inspiring leaders, Mahatma Gandhi, Martin Luther King Jr., Saint Teresa (among my personal favorites), I find a common thread emerges: They all put aside personal goals and instead passionately embraced the causes and needs of the people they served.

Over the course of my career, I've seen and worked with my share of bad – some horrendous – corporate leaders. Usually, these CEOs or presidents came on board organizations and failed to convincingly "live" or exemplify the organization's missions and goals. They failed to make that special connection with both managers and employees. This same scenario applies to senior executive leaders as well. They fail to inspire their staff and mid-managers because they're unable to impart feelings of unity and excitement.

So what makes a great leader? If you are currently responsible for leading a company, or you envision yourself someday climbing up the corporate ladder and taking a senior executive role, consider these tips:

Be a great communicator. At every opportunity, talk about the vision of greatness you see for your company, not just the mind-numbing details of quarterly goals or how you're meeting expectations from investors or your parent company. Think about the great leaders in history who have had to mobilize countries (Franklin Delano Roosevelt during the Great Depression and then World War II) or recreate companies (Lee Iacocca, who revived the Chrysler Corporation as its CEO in the 1980s). They were visionaries!

But what made them uniquely special is that they excelled at communication at all levels. In today's world, communication has accelerated, with many different avenues available. A strong leader with good communication skills must be able to transcend all communication mediums, including social media, traditional media, employee coffee-talks and mass communication.

Thread your organization's mission statement and cultural beliefs into everything you say and do. If you can do this successfully, and master all forms of communication opportunities, you will get others to see and believe in that vision. Plus, your employees will come to appreciate your positive outlook and clarity of message, and they'll work harder to make your vision a reality.

Let your personality shine through. You can be a good communicator, but if you're a cold fish, you're going to have difficulty getting people excited and lined up behind you. Bring the same personality you wear at home to the workplace. You can help inspire people by relaxing, being yourself and by conveying that "we're all in this together." When you expose your humanity to employees, it only makes you more endearing. However, you can't reveal too much information with those you lead, for example, intimate details about your private life or your political beliefs. I've known leaders who've let their professional lives bleed into their personal lives. I've often felt this was "TMI" (too much information). When that happens, respect goes out the window. Maintain those professional boundaries!

Be passionate. If you're not committed and passionate to your causes, you won't get employees to support it. There's no room for being disingenuous – you either believe it or you don't. Some companies and boards make a big mistake when they hire a new CEO that comes in and merely repeats the company line. That's a disservice to employees and the whole company because whoever hires isn't gauging the candidate's level of passion – even if their resume screams "qualified." The new-hire executive winds up going out there and being a talking head. They don't believe what they're saying themselves. So they're not exhibiting passion for their job, company or staff. If you're not passionate about the company and the product or people you're leading, you're going to have a very difficult time getting people to march forward with you. Renowned Chinese philosopher Lao Tzu said: "To lead people, walk behind them." On many occasions, I've personally found that statement to be true.

Don't be a bully. Hey, this is America, we want to be inspired by our leaders – not obey and follow orders simply because they're in high office. In the workplace, autocratic leaders may see success in, say, meeting deadlines or getting things done. But they usually can't totally win over the hearts and minds of their employees. I know plenty of colleagues who've put their time in with autocrats, only to eventually leave their management positions because their CEO or managing executive knew only one way of doing things – their own way. Yes, you can have convictions, but collaboration and diversity of ideas produce great innovation and, at the same time, make management and employees feel like they're contributing and part of the process.

Walk the talk. The biggest lesson I've learned over the years about leadership is that you can't be a "Do as I say, not as I do" leader. People do not respect that at all. It's actually very demoralizing to management and employees. You'll see your support erode rapidly. As a leader, you can expect some degree of respect based on your title. But you have to earn the rest. And walking the talk is how you get it. I've left a few jobs in my career because I was disappointed senior leaders weren't doing this. In this age, where companies have to compete for great employees, you can't afford to have leadership that is not walking the talk.

Be humble. A leader has to be able to admit mistakes and errors in judgment – plus apologize for them. Your employees will admire you for it, and they'll line up behind you in support. Conversely, senior leaders who don't acknowledge errors and apologize, and instead just hope that people will forget about them, make a mistake that affects the companies and departments they lead. Employees and management will emulate that behavior, and soon enough no one will take ownership and responsibility for mistakes and judgment errors. It is a downward spiral from that point onward.

My Leadership Moment

When I think about my days as President & CEO of the National Business Travel Association (now the Global Business Travel Association), I recall some of the most challenging days of my life and career. The organization was at a critical survival juncture. The balance sheet was not healthy, and the U.S. and global economies turned upside down when terrorists attacked New York and Washington, D.C., on September 11, 2001. People stopped traveling and meeting, and that devastated many businesses, especially the airline and hospitality industries. At the same time, I was named as one of the lead integration managers to work on the merger between Compaq and Hewlett-Packard, where I was senior global category manager on the Global Travel & Meetings team.

But that was a very rewarding and self-affirming time, too. Despite the challenges, I felt my "leadership moment," a concept I learned from Michael Useem, who is the William and Jacalyn Egan Professor of Management at The Wharton School, University of Pennsylvania. A leadership moment is when it sinks in that you have to dig down deep and focus on the greater good for everyone, pushing aside your fear or your desire for personal glory. The decisions you make as a leader can make or break a situation, and sometimes they can lead to loss of life and other catastrophic results.

Michael Useem states it best in the introduction to his book, *The Leadership Moment: Nine True Stories of Triumph and Disaster and Their Lessons for Us All*[xiii]: "Leadership is at its best when the vision is strategic, the voice persuasive, the results tangible."

I believe that good leaders think on behalf of the company … the nation … the world and put their personal agendas aside. And, like Gandhi and Martin Luther King, Jr., they apply their own experiences overcoming hardships to serve others. If you've been through hard times in your life, use those experiences to empathize with your employees. Forget yourself, and focus on your leadership responsibilities.

When I look back at the leadership moment decisions I made as President and CEO for the GBTA, I can confidently say I focused on putting others first. I, along with the Board of Directors, promoted the greater good for the benefit of the association and the business travel ecosystem. The cumulative results speak for themselves. GBTA today is a real success story; they are stronger than ever, not just financially, but also in how they execute their vision and mission for the organization and the members they serve. I think my parents would be proud. I took to heart a fundamental principle they taught me as a child – to make decisions that benefit others versus me. They told me that, by doing so, I could not make a bad decision.

My experience at GBTA also helped me make a career out of crisis management. I did my best to not let present events affect my ability to get things done. And I also learned that, to successfully manage through a crisis, you need to collaborate with your co-workers and fellow executives. We never do it alone.

Think about it. You can be afraid of chaos or you can look upon it as an opportunity. It's a chance to get things done that normally would take a lot of time and meet with a lot of resistance. I'm thankful I learned that, during tumultuous times, the winning formula is to remain calm, communicate, collaborate and then lead others along the path to higher ground.

Mentoring – Rewarding for All Involved

> "Before you are a leader, success is all about
> growing yourself. When you become a leader,
> success is all about growing others."
> --Jack Welch

In its simplest definition, mentoring is when you give help or advice to a person who is less experienced (often younger) than you because you genuinely want to see that person grow in their professional or personal life.

Mentoring can be frustrating – especially when your mentee makes a bad decision because they ignored your advice or failed to follow through on a suggestion. But mentoring can also be a most rewarding experience, as you watch that person adopt more productive behavior, reach new goals and receive recognition for their successes.

I've had several mentors in my life in the various jobs I've held, but one very special person stands out in my mind – Catherine "Cass" MacMullin. She was the travel manager with Ernst & Young in Los Angeles, and she was also the chapter president for the Los Angeles Business Travel Association (LABTA).

When I met Cass, I was a new supplier member of LABTA, working in sales for Northwest Airlines. For whatever reason, she took a shine to me. I was very green, and here was this person who was a leader of the local chapter, as well as a committee leader at the National Business Travel Association (NBTA) – which is today the Global Business Travel Association (GBTA). She thought I had volunteer leadership potential and singled me out for personal attention. I was humbled and honored that she saw something in me, and that prompted me to believe that maybe I, too, could earn a chapter leadership role.

Years later, I was elected President of LABTA, ironically in a year when the NBTA's national convention was being held in Los Angeles. So as chapter President, my Board of Directors and chapter volunteer leaders had to work with the NBTA staff to coordinate logistical support, volunteers, etc. The conference was a tremendous success and got me noticed by the NBTA leadership, who eventually asked me to chair several industry committees.

6 Tips for Successful Mentoring

1. *From the outset, make sure your mentee is open and willing to accept advice and constructive feedback.*
2. *Create an environment where you and your mentee can be candid, non-emotional and non-judgmental. Doing this is essential for keeping things honest and constructive.*
3. *Listen well and don't be a bully; be supportive.*
4. *Make sure you discuss disagreements of opinion face-to-face. Until you can do a sit-down, give your mentee the benefit of the doubt that they mean no harm.*
5. *Know your time limits. Make sure you're not getting over-committed to the point where you're neglecting your own work and responsibilities.*
6. *Cut mentees loose if they're being defensive and not following your advice or suggestions.*

That led to even bigger things. I ran for a position on the Board, where I served three two-year terms as Vice President, President and CEO and then Chairman Past-President.

Sadly, Cass never saw me become president of LABTA, nor my election to the Executive Board of Directors for GBTA. Tragically, she died suddenly, which was a shock to us all. She gave me encouragement, and I'll always be grateful for her generosity of time and unconditional support. Even after all these years and after my career milestones, the impact of her mentorship still resonates and guides me today. I hope she's smiling down from heaven, and I hope she is proud that her investment and belief in me was justified.

Be a Cheerleader

Over the course of my career, I've mentored about a dozen people, and what's really special is that many of them still reach out to me for advice or to just check in. That's very touching! It gives me a chance to catch up with them, find out how they're doing and continue to be of service. I'm also proud to say that all of my mentees have achieved great success in their lives and careers. Even today I continue to be their cheerleader.

I met my first mentee very early in my career, when I was a sales manager at Northwest Airlines. Through the years I even had the privilege of mentoring colleagues who've gone on to become GBTA and Association of Corporate Travel Executives (ACTE) presidents. And, even though I am semi-retired, I continue to mentor. Mentoring gives me the most satisfying feeling of accomplishment.

Recently, I met some former engineering colleagues from StarCite for coffee. When we first met, they were talented engineers. Today they're currently in senior leadership roles, overseeing engineers for two start-ups in Silicon Valley. They asked me to mentor them, and I was very touched. Of course, I agreed. As they put it, they wanted to follow my example and become "inspirational executives," to "lead by example and inspiration versus the usual intimidation style most leaders exhibit." How could I turn down a request like that?

There are a lot of things you can do for a mentee. Number one on my list: Be their biggest cheerleader. You have to give them unqualified support and encouragement. At the same time, create a relationship where you can be honest and give them transparent and constructive feedback. It's crucial, too, to foster an atmosphere of trust. When your mentees come to you complaining about their jobs or someone they report to or work with, you have to keep whatever is shared absolutely confidential.

Cass was my biggest cheerleader. Once, at lunch, she committed to helping me work through something, and I looked at her and said: "How can I ever repay you?" She answered: "You just have to do the same for others. That generosity and kindness will come back to you tenfold."

Putting in the time and support for another pays off. When you see your mentee become successful, it brings you a tremendous sense of satisfaction and joy. And for me that's worth so much more than a big bonus or raise. And Cass was absolutely right about paying it forward. I can't begin to add up the times others have been kind and generous to me throughout my career. It's very reassuring to know that so many people are paying it forward.

Perhaps the highest compliment someone can pay you as a mentor is that you're generous with your time. And, if you're getting that feedback a lot, it means you're consistent in your personal brand. It proves that, whatever you're doing to develop and maintain your personal brand, it's working!

> "What I think the mentor gets is the great satisfaction of helping somebody along, helping somebody take advantage of an opportunity that maybe he or she did not have."
> — CLINT EASTWOOD

AFTERWORD

"Your work is going to fill a large part of your life, and
the only way to be truly satisfied is to do what you
believe is great work. And the only way to do great
work is to love what you do. If you haven't found it
yet, keep looking. Don't settle. As with all matters
of the heart, you'll know when you find it."

— STEVE JOBS

This book was on my "to do" list for many years. It started as an idea from someone I was mentoring who casually said to me: "You have such great career philosophy and advice. You should write a book about the importance of personal brand."

Fast forward six years later. Here we are.

My main objective for writing this book is to offer some advice and guidance to people starting out in their careers or who've reached a crossroad in their professional lives. I'm continually honored and privileged to get requests from industry professionals seeking advice on managing their careers and balancing their personal and professional lives.

In May 2016, I chose to slow down and focus more on my personal life and projects (such as this book) that I had put on the back burner. So, I officially semi-retired from Lanyon, where I spent the last few years as Vice President of Industry Strategy.

I'm still busy with my projects, family, friends and playing with my dog, Kimo. And I've stayed involved with my industry blog, media articles and op-eds. I'm also committed to various industry boards on which I sit, and I do some select consulting projects.

My biggest regret is that I just don't have enough time to mentor as many people as I would like. Hopefully the lessons I've learned throughout my career and the advice I've offered in this book will help many people achieve and exceed their professional goals, as well as realize the importance of authenticity, consistency and solid leadership. I believe people are often already aware of these principles. They just need a reminder to keep them on the right path to success and fulfillment.

I want to thank my editor and collaborator for this book, Don Munro. Don is a very talented writer and the best collaborative partner anyone could wish for in terms of his honesty, hard work and writing/editing talents. I think it's fair to say he makes me appear to be smarter than I really am!

Warm thanks, too, to Katharine Williams, Director of Marketing at GoldSpring Consulting, who very generously helped review this manuscript.

I also want to sincerely thank my family and relatives for their unfailing support: Kimo and Stephen; Ann and Floyd; Carole and Eddie; Vi, Wayne and John. I owe much gratitude to my sisters and their families: Gayle, Chris, Ryan and Brandon Wong; Joi, Mike and Michelle Muranaka; and Mathew, Janelle, Lincoln and Liam Muranaka.

Thank you for taking the time to read about my career journey and my quest for personal brand integrity. I truly hope it will inspire you to do great things and be a positive influence over people in your personal and professional circles.

I believe we all hunger for inner fulfillment. It's part of what drives us as human beings. My fundamental truth, first taught to me all those years ago by my parents, Richard and Amy Iwamoto, has been to treat people like I wanted them to treat me. I've tried to spend my career bringing that priceless advice to life and pay my blessings forward. I urge you to do the same—it will bring you more satisfaction than a title or compensation.

Most importantly, spend your life loving what you do! Be passionate about everything and everyone in it.

Kevin Iwamoto

NOTES

i   Survey conducted online within the United States by Harris Poll on behalf of University of Phoenix® School of Business from April 3-7, 2015 among 2,032 U.S. adults, ages 18 and older, 1,084 who identified as either currently employed or looking for work.

ii   "NYSE President: I Owe Every Job I've Ever Had to Networking," (http://fortune.com/2015/07/07/tom-farley-networking-tips/) *Fortune*, July 7, 2015

iii   Source: Facebook. Facebook had 1.13 billion daily active users on average for June 2016.

iv   Source: Twitter. Twitter had approximately 313 million monthly active users as of June 30, 2016.

v   Source: LinkedIn. LinkedIn operates the world's largest professional network on the Internet with more than 450 million registered members in over 200 countries and territories.

vi   *Mobile Messaging and Social Media 2015* (http://www.pewinternet.org/2015/08/19/mobile-messaging-and-social-media-2015/), Pew Research Center.

vii   *Meetings & Conventions Industry Insights* (http://www.meetings conventions.com//Blogs/IndustryInsights/)

viii   "The 12 Dos & Don'ts of Using Facebook for Business," (http://blog.hubspot.com/marketing/dos-donts-facebook-business-infographic#sm.00f kwbnc17yuers11s91gs3iq6hat), November 16, 2015

ix   *2015 Jobvite Recruiter Nation Survey* (http://www.jobvite.com/press-releases/2015/jobvites-new-2015-recruiter-nation-survey-reveals-talent-crunch/)

[x] Salary.com's (http://www1.salary.com/Six-Sigma-Black-Belt-Salaries.html) Certified Compensation Professionals analyzed survey data collected from thousands of HR departments at companies of all sizes and industries to present a range of annual salaries for people with the job title Six Sigma Black Belt in the United States.

[xi] PCMA *Convene's 2016 Salary Survey* (http://www.pcmaconvene.org/features/salary-survey/convenes-2016-salary-survey/) was conducted by Lewis&Clark, lewisclarkinc.com, and sponsored by DMAI's empowerMINT.com.

[xii] "Women in Elite Jobs Face Stubborn Pay Gap," *The Wall Street Journal,* May 17, 2016. The publication analyzed Census Bureau earnings data for full-time, year-round workers – across 446 major occupations – from 2010 through 2014.

[xiii] Useem, Michael. *The Leadership Moment: Nine True Stories of Triumph and Disaster and Their Lessons for Us All.* New York: Three Rivers, 1998. Print.